PRAYING THROUGH THE LORD'S PRAYER

Praying

THROUGH THE

Lord's Prayer

STEVE HARPER

UPPER
ROOM BOOKS
NASHVILLE

Praying through the Lord's Prayer

Cover Design: C. J. Helms
First Printing: April 1992 (7)
Second Printing: May 1993 (5)
Library of Congress Catalog Card Number: 91-67166
ISBN: 0-8358-0656-1

Printed in the United States of America

"Our Father" . . .
is an address of intimacy,
centered in the belief that God cares
about the totality of our lives.

STEVE HARPER

Contents

Introduction   9

Chapter One—PRAYER: WHO? ME?   13

Chapter Two—PRAYER: HERE?   27

Chapter Three—PRAYER: NOW?   39

Chapter Four—PRAYER: ABOUT *THIS*?   53

Chapter Five—PRAYER: LIKE THIS?   69

Chapter Six—READY TO GO!   83

Additional Resources   103

Introduction

The Apostle Paul described the Christian life as a race (Acts 20:24). I like that image. Races are exhilarating. But the idea also includes struggle. Racing can leave us breathless, sometimes bordering on exhaustion. Every racer knows that at some point during a race there is a critical need for "second wind." In fact, a "second wind" often determines whether or not a runner will finish a race.

Prayer is one aspect of the Christian race. For me, it is like running the hurdles in a track race. I do not go far before I must leap over some obstacle that would otherwise break my stride and prevent me from finishing as I should. These "prayer hurdles" line the track from beginning to end. They are never completely out of the picture.

The Lord's Prayer helps us leap some of the common "prayer hurdles," or obstacles to prayer. Until recently, I had never thought of the Lord's Prayer as a way Jesus used to help the disciples overcome obstacles to prayer. This insight can make the Lord's Prayer even more valuable as a means of teaching us how to pray.

In giving us the Lord's Prayer, Jesus gave us both the "first wind" and "second wind" of prayer to enable us to keep running and to finish the Christian race. The "first wind" of prayer comes through a study of the various terms and phrases of the prayer itself. An understanding of the meaning of the prayer can greatly assist us as we begin or continue a life of prayer. Thus, we can speak of the "first wind" as the pattern for prayer that the Lord's Prayer provides. This is the framework out of which this book is written. The last chapter in particular addresses directly the use of the Lord's Prayer as a basic pattern for prayer.

But the Lord's Prayer also gives us the "second wind" of prayer. It helps us deal with some of the questions that arise in relation to vital praying. Until recently, I had never thought of the prayer in this way. But now I see that Jesus was not only giving a pattern for prayer, he was also giving a kind of psychology for prayer. Or, to put it another way, in the "first wind" he was giving the meaning, the message, the *substance* of prayer. In the "second wind" he was giving the *spirit* of prayer and the motivation for praying.

As we develop more deeply a life grounded in prayer, motivation becomes a critical factor. Desire, much more than technique, is that which sustains vital prayer. There are plenty of "how to's" if we can keep alive the "want to." In the Lord's Prayer I see Jesus having touched upon important questions that serve to keep alive a motivation to pray, to maintain the intimacy of a relationship with God that is implied in the *Abba* form by which Jesus addressed God in the Lord's Prayer.

I want this book to be for you a source of inspiration as you run the Christian race where you live and work. The hurdles, the obstacles, are there. The times when we cannot finish the race unless we attain a "second wind" are very real and sometimes painful times. But through the Lord's Prayer, Jesus has enabled us to see that the obstacles can be overcome and the near–breaking points do not have to stop us or defeat us.

As you read these chapters and engage in the questions and reflective exercises, I pray that you will experience a renewal of joy and effectiveness in your prayer life as you more often and more deeply pray through the Lord's Prayer.

Chapter One

Prayer: Who? Me?

After the opening hymn had been sung at the Sunday evening services, I spoke from the pulpit to our lay leader and asked, "Wayne, will you offer a prayer for us?" Without hesitation, he said, "No." When the service was over, I went straight to Wayne and apologized, thinking his refusal was due to my catching him off guard and unprepared. But his response was different. He said, "I didn't pray because that is what you're supposed to do as the preacher." And as long as I was his pastor, Wayne never changed his mind.

The idea that prayer is for special people erodes the motive for prayer. I have seen this idea in operation over and over in the lives of people. For some of us it is a notion that goes back as far as we can remember.

Bob had come out of a tradition where "real" praying was done by professional clergy. He might pray on the run now and then, but when he really wanted his requests to get through, he asked his pastor to pray for him. He didn't think his own prayers had the same kind of power.

Mary's problem was different. Her hesitancy to pray stemmed from her growing up in a church where the only laity who ever prayed publicly were the "prayer warriors." By this I mean the people who were best known for their ability to pray aloud before a group. Mary certainly did not see herself in that light, so she approached her praying with tentativeness and lack of confidence.

Fred did not hesitate to tell me why he stayed away from Sunday School. "I am afraid they might call on me to pray, and I just clam up whenever I have to talk in front of people." My assurances that we could alert his teacher and thus avoid possible embarrassment to him were not enough to overcome his fear of having to pray in public.

These kinds of stories reveal the tendency in people to paint a picture of prayer as an exercise for those who are especially spiritual or those who are professionally trained. What a different picture is painted when we turn to the Lord's Prayer. The prayer was given in response to the request, "Lord, teach us to pray."

And who are the "us"? They are the

disciples, none of whom were professionally trained, but instead were fishermen, tax collectors, and political revolutionaries. They are the women who followed and the "common people" who gladly heard Jesus. They are the ordinary folk. They are the kind of people you and I are.

If prayer had been limited to special people, Jesus would never have given the Lord's Prayer. Instead, he would have answered, "You don't need to learn how to pray. Just tell me what you want, and I will pray for you." After all, Jesus was the Son of God. Surely, if anyone could get through to God, he could. In fact, Luke tells us that Jesus had just finished praying when the disciples made their request. If it had been inappropriate, Jesus could have cleared that up once and for all. If their desire to learn to pray was some kind of second-class request, he could have come right out and said so. Instead, he responded positively to the disciples.

In both instances where the Lord's Prayer is given, Matthew 6 and Luke 11, Jesus indicated that prayer is for everyone. He did not hesitate to instruct the disciples in vital praying. In Matthew he responded, "This is how you should pray" (6:9). And in Luke he said, "When you pray, say: . . ." (11:21). Jesus wants us to know there is no hierarchy of prayer, that prayer is for everyone. As our prayers wing their way toward the heart of God, there is no distinction between "first class" and "coach."

I still recall when this hit me with full force, I was pastoring a country church during seminary. Jeannie and I had been invited to a member's home for lunch. In Kentucky that means a "family feast." The table was piled high and as many places as possible were set around it. When we were all together, the hostess called on the youngest child to pray. Immediately and dutifully, the little girl bowed her head, folded her hands, closed her eyes, and said,

> God is great, and God is good.
> Let us thank Him for our food.
> By His hands we all are fed.
> Thank you for our daily bread. Amen.

No sooner had the child finished than the hostess looked at me and said, "And now, preacher, would you ask the blessing for us?" In that moment, the little girl and I made eye contact. I will never forget the puzzled expression on her face. She looked at me as if to say, "I thought I just did that."

In those days I was still too caught up in "correct" pastoral duties and responses, and, frankly, the woman's request took me by surprise. So, I prayed. But even as I did, there was an uneasiness in my heart. Even though my eyes were closed, I could still see the child's little face. If I had been wiser then, I would have said, "Why, there's no need for another prayer. We just had a great prayer." And we had.

Prayer Is for Everyone

There are no "toy prayers." Every prayer is genuine, and every prayer receives the attention of our heavenly Father. That is the first hurdle the Lord's Prayer helps us leap. Prayer is not just for special people; it is for everyone. It is important that we get this point across as clearly as we can and as soon as we can.

Let's begin with our children. If we retain childhood memories of specific "prayer warriors" —memories that make us hesitant to pray aloud in groups or that make us doubt the effectiveness of our prayers—that is all the proof we need to address this issue with our children when they are young. Early impressions fall on innocent soil and can reap a positive or negative harvest for years to come.

Susanna Wesley was a believer in teaching children to pray at an early age. In fact, before the Wesley children could speak, they were taught to make signs with their hands during prayer. It may have been something as simple as folding them, or it may have been something like the sign of the cross. But even before words and speaking, the children were brought into the prayer life of the Wesley family. As they grew older, they were involved as was appropriate. No child was excluded.

This truth came to our home in an unexpected way. We have the custom of joining hands and bowing our heads during the blessing. I always end the prayer by saying, "In Jesus' name." One evening, before I could get the usual "Amen" out, our baby daughter said, "Amen!" We all jumped at the sound of her voice. Without any particular instructions, Katrina had discovered that *Amen* was the word which comes after "In Jesus' name." From that moment on, she became our "Amen girl." At prayer times, I (or whoever was praying) would say, "In Jesus' name" and then pause for Katrina to belt out a hearty "Amen!"

Another way to communicate that prayer is for everyone, is to accept everyone's prayer as important and authentic. This takes some flexibility when working with children (and even adults!), but this acceptance is essential. One night as we tucked John into bed, we asked him if there was anyone he wanted to pray for. He answered, "Yes. I want to pray for Bert and

Ernie." A devout "Sesame Street" TV-viewer in those days, he wanted to pray for his buddies.

When John said that, something in my adult mind said, *He shouldn't pray for that; Bert and Ernie aren't real.* But, thank God, those words never reached my lips. For they were checked by another thought that said, *Wait a minute! They are real to John. Bert and Ernie are as much a part of John's world as graduate school is to yours.* And so, we knelt down by the side of the bed and prayed that God would bless Bert and Ernie.

The misconception about prayer's special-ness is almost always couched in the realm of verbal prayer. We can communicate that prayer is for everyone by allowing a person's prayer to be either silent or spoken. This takes into consideration those of us who become catatonic at the thought of having to say anything in a group. It enables us to silently pray a prayer that is more personal and private than spoken prayer allows. It permits us to join in the spirit of prayer when we have nothing new to add but wish to pray with the group.

All these are legitimate reasons for not always praying aloud. And in communicating prayer's reality, we should affirm the validity of silent as well as spoken prayer. Prayer is ulti-mately the language of the heart.

Feeling Comfortable with Prayer

Even though I teach prayer in a theological school, there are many times when I will not pray aloud in a group, simply to communicate the idea that it is OK to participate silently in the prayer process.

I developed many of my ideas about prayer during the time when the small-group movement was in full swing in congregations during the late 1960s and early 1970s. One feature of the groups was the "prayer circle." Usually at the end of a time of Bible study or personal sharing, the prayer circle was the climax of the whole experience. One by one we would go around the circle until *everyone* had prayed. Notice that I said *everyone.*

It was not unusual for someone in the group to feel very ill at ease. I can remember some prayers that were spoken so softly they could hardly be heard or mumbled in a way they could not be understood. I remember prayers that were stumbled over, to the embarrassment of the one trying to pray. And I remember conversations with people who became very discouraged after such faltering attempts—people who were left to feel that they would never learn to "really pray."

Then one day, Bruce Larson and Keith Miller came to the rescue when they began to teach that it's OK to "pass" in prayer circles. By saying this they connected the contemporary prayer-and-share movement with historic Christianity, salvaging the much-needed truth that prayer does not have to be spoken in order to be genuine. In the process Larson and Miller liberated many people.

The writings of G. Ernest Thomas have also helped me in this regard. Dr. Thomas was an experienced teacher of prayer to professional people. Along the way, he had observed that many of them had never prayed aloud in a group before, even though they might have spoken in public to large crowds. In addition to the "It's OK to pass" principle, Dr. Thomas encouraged growth in prayer in two ways. First, he always had prayer books available on the table. He would tell the persons, "If you don't feel comfortable praying extemporaneously, look through one of the books until you find a prayer that communicates what you want to say. Then, during your turn, read it to us."

Second, he would encourage people to bring pencil and paper to the prayer group. During the course of the meeting he would ask those who were not comfortable praying "on the spot" to write out several sentences that expressed their ideas and feelings. Then, in turn, each person could read what he or she had written. Over the years, many people testified that one of Dr. Thomas' methods led them to a meaningful prayer life, especially when praying in a small group.

There is good precedent for this in the Wesleyan tradition. One of John Wesley's earliest devotional habits was "collecting prayers." Just as some people collect stamps, he collected prayers. Wesley would carefully copy these prayers into his devotional manual. When someone came to him asking for help in learning to pray, he would make a copy of his collected prayers and give them to his seeking friend. It was Wesley's conviction that the best way to teach persons how to pray was to expose them to the prayers of others. By carefully examining these prayers, one would discover the content, spirit, and vocabulary of vital prayer.

Along the same line, I have discovered two more ways that have been very useful in enlisting others to pray.

The first came in connection with my pastoral visitation. I become frustrated with always being the one to pray aloud during a pastoral call. So, I began to ask the person whom I was visiting to pray for me, in addition to the praying I was doing for them. This not only enriched the quality of our conversation, it also set the stage for some of the most moving and memorable praying experiences I have had.

The second idea has come more recently. I have discovered that some people are visually inspired. Based on this, I will often display a painting or photograph and ask the group to meditate on the image until a prayer is formed in their hearts and minds. I have been surprised and moved by the prayers which have emerged in response to what we were looking at.

Prayer is for everyone. The Lord's Prayer teaches us that. Jesus leaves out no follower. Jesus invites everyone to pray. Not everyone can or should pray alike. And no one should be given the impression that true prayer has to be made in any single way. It does not. But everyone can pray.

If you have trouble accepting your own praying as being equally valid to that of the prayer warriors you have known, hear Jesus' words "When you pray. . . ." as our Lord's invitation into a life of vital prayer. As a prayer exercise, take the phrases printed at the top of the following page. Read them over and commit them to memory. Then, repeat these phrases throughout the day until the Lord's invitation sinks into your mind and heart.

Jesus invites me to pray.
Jesus wants me to pray.
Jesus waits to hear and answer my prayer.

Harry Emerson Fosdick called prayer a "native tendency" of the human being. By that he meant we are created to pray. In addition to the invitation phrases above, think back to the times when you *know* you have prayed. What did you pray about? What words or thoughts did you use in praying? These kinds of questions are important to remind yourself that prayer is not something you are beginning; it is something you are improving. You have already prayed; everyone prays. Whenever you catch yourself thinking, *Is prayer for me?*, know that the only answer is "You bet!"

On the basis of that assurance, what one concern would you like to pray for right now?

Now, as a closing act to this chapter, write several sentences that turn this concern into a simple prayer to God.

Questions for Discussion
Chapter One

1. Do you have any experiences in your past which have tempted you to believe that prayer is only for "special" people?

2. If you have overcome this idea of exclusiveness of prayer, how did you do so? Do you still struggle with this notion? In what ways?

3. What difference does it make to know that Jesus invites, even desires, us to pray?

4. What experiences—past or present—have you had in which the example of ordinary people has inspired or helped you in your own prayer life?

Prayer: Here?

The secretary pointed to the telephone receiver. "Dr. Mayfield is calling long distance. He wants to talk with you," she said. She motioned for me to go into his office, where I could take the call in private. Dr. Mayfield and I talked for a few minutes about the General Conference of The United Methodist Church that he was attending as a delegate. As we came to the end of our conversation, he said to me, "Before we hang up, let's pray." That was the first time I had prayed over the telephone.

Dan ran a service station in Wilmore during the week. But nearly every weekend, he was preaching in a rural Kentucky church. He usually took one of the seminarians with him. In time, my turn came. As we rode along, Dan said, "We're getting close to the church; we'd better start praying." Then, without skipping a breath, he began to pray aloud while driving down the highway. That was the first time I had ever prayed aloud in a car.

A close friend wrote me a letter. In it he indicated he was praying for me. As the final paragraph of the letter, he had written out the prayer he was praying on my behalf. Then, he simply ended the letter with "Your friend, Tommy." That was the first time I had been prayed for in a letter.

I share these stories because when each of them occurred, I was struck by the "unusual" place in which each prayer was made. If we are to maintain a life of prayer, it is essential for us to learn that prayer is not an activity reserved for special places. Prayer is for anyplace.

Prayer Places

When Jesus gave the disciples the Lord's Prayer, he was not in a special place. In both instances where the prayer was given, the place was quite ordinary. In Matthew it was on a mountain. In Luke, it appears that Jesus and the disciples were on the road, journeying from one place to another. By instructing the disciples about prayer in these ordinary places, Jesus was teaching that anyplace is a good place to pray.

Our Lord confirmed this by his own example. Luke tells us that Jesus had just finished praying in this ordinary place. The Gospels further reveal Jesus praying in private and in public. He prayed in the Temple and in the synagogues. He prayed in homes and on the open road. He prayed at funerals and at parties. He prayed in the Garden of Gethsemane, and he prayed from the cross. He prayed in nearly all the possible locations of his time.

This truth in no way detracts from the significance of holy places. All of us have had the privilege to be in places where the atmosphere was saturated with the prayers of the faithful and in which it was easy to be drawn into a spirit of prayer. I believe in holy places. I use some of those places regularly in my prayer life. I believe the church is indeed a "house of prayer" and that the prayers of God's people should go forth from there.

But I am equally glad that prayer is not confined to those places. Often I am miles from a special place when the need for prayer is apparent. How wonderful to see that prayer is as real in a supermarket as in a cathedral!

In 1973 I had the privilege of going to India with Dr. J. T. Seamands. About twenty of us were journeying with this veteran missionary, and in a month's time we experienced unforgettable things. One evening we traveled to the outskirts of Bombay called "the hutment." It was a slum area where thousands of people had used pieces of tin and cardboard to construct simple housing. They were rural people who had fled from severe drought, hoping to find food and work in the city.

The church was at work in the hutment. We were invited to attend a dedication service, Dr. Seamands did not tell us any more than that. We boarded our vans and headed out of the city. When we arrived at our destination, we entered a home no larger than an average-sized room in most houses in the United States. We learned that sixty-four people lived there. By the time we arrived, the room was filled, except for the space the people had reserved for us. Numerous friends and neighbors stood outside. Still, all we knew was that we were attending a dedication service.

Someone had brought an old portable field organ. We sang hymns and choruses, celebrating the presence of God in this home and in our hearts. At last, the time came for the actual dedication. Only at the last minute did any of us realize what we were dedicating—a light bulb. Not a light fixture; a light bulb. It was a bulb dangling at the end of a cord in the middle of the room. This was the first night the little house had had light inside. The Christians who lived there wanted us to come and praise God with them for their new light bulb. They would now be able to see in their home after dark.

Of all the places I have been on the earth, no place has ever excelled that room as a place of prayer. Through blurred eyes and with voices tightened by emotion, we sang the Doxology. Dr. Seamands prayed the prayer of dedication for that light bulb. And the glory of God filled that place as surely as the new light filled it. *Anyplace is a good place to pray.*

Ask those who were prisoners of war in the Viet Nam era, or POWs from any other war. The testimony is consistent—they communed with God in their prison cells under the worst of conditions. Many of them state frankly that if the presence of God had not been there, they would never have made it. Anyplace is a good place to pray.

Perhaps my best teacher in this respect was Dr. Frank C. Laubach. In his book *Prayer: The Mightiest Force in the World,* he introduced me to the idea of "flash prayers." Dr. Laubach had practiced this type of prayer for years, often with amazing results.

The idea is simple. No matter where you are, you can pray. Whenever Dr. Laubach saw a person for whom he was moved to pray, he would simply call the name of "Jesus" in his mind and then either the name of the person, or the condition of the person. For example, he would pray, "Jesus, friend—Jesus is coming to you." Or he might pray, "Jesus—the homeless person." "Jesus—the distraught mother." Each day provided literally hundreds of opportunities to pray like that. For him, the day was, from beginning to end, a continuous prayer time.

The theology behind this kind of praying is sound. It is an expression of our belief in the ever-present God and the Lordship of Christ. This belief was powerfully communicated to me by an elderly member of the first church I served after seminary graduation. Mrs. Parker was one of my best supporters. Throughout my tenure in Roby, Texas, she was in my "cheering section." After learning that I would be appointed to another church, I began my last round of pastoral calls.

When I came to Mrs. Parker, among other things, what I wanted to know from her was the foundation of her faith. I wanted to know what had sustained her for so long, despite several tragedies and numerous setbacks. I wanted to know what had kept a twinkle in her eyes. With no hesitation Mrs. Parker answered, "I have been sustained by this one truth: Wherever I am, God is."

In giving the disciples the Lord's Prayer on the mountain and on the road, Jesus was teaching the same lesson. He was telling the disciples that there was no place they could go where God would not be present. Just before he ascended into heaven, the Master reminded them of the same truth when he said, "Remember, I am with you always" (Matt. 28:29). That truth has sustained the saints for twenty centuries.

Saint Augustine found God in a garden; Saint Francis of Assisi, in the face of leper. Julian of Norwich encountered God during intense illness. Martin Luther met God while standing before the Diet of Worms. John Wesley's life was changed in a small-group meeting on Aldersgate Street in London. And Mother Teresa sees Christ in the faces of the dying on the streets of Calcutta.

Here is the principle we need to take to heart: It is not the place that sanctifies the prayer; it is the prayer that sanctifies the place. For it is in prayer that we recognize and acknowledge that God is not limited to certain locations. The old gospel song is right; God is "only a prayer away"!

Across the years of my ministry, I have had the joy of seeing this truth dawn on people. I remember the seminary student who discovered he could pray in the cab of his truck. I recall the physician who trained himself to pray for each new patient as he or she walked through the examining room door. I rejoiced with the telephone operator who found every long-distance caller to be a person for whom to pray. I will never forget the public school teacher who told me she arrived before any of her students just so she could pray for the place where each would be sitting during the day.

"Wherever I am, God is."

Finding a Place to Pray

If anyplace is a good place to pray, then I need to do at least two things. First, I need to become more consciously aware of the places that fill my days. Henri Nouwen was once asked to give a simple definition of the spiritual life. He responded, "paying attention." When I read his words, I thought of how often I had failed to sense and connect with the presence of God because I was not really paying attention to my surroundings.

What are the places that fill your life? Who are the people in those places? Begin to get in touch with them, one by one. Stop long enough to let each location and each individual stand out specifically and individually. It is when we begin to see life like this that we begin to experience the vision of God. God does not see *en masse* but, rather, sees each individual object and person. Jesus said that not even a single sparrow falls to the ground without God's knowledge (see Matthew 10:29-31 and Luke 12:6-7).

Recall Jesus' words about the final judgment as recorded in Matthew 25. The difference is not that one group did good and another, evil. The difference is that one group did good and the other group did nothing. In fact, their question to the Lord is "When did we see you . . .?" (Matt. 25:44) The root of their sin lay in their blindness, in their being oblivious to their surroundings and opportunities.

Making every place a place of prayer means beginning to pay attention to the places which fill up our days. In my case, it is the classrooms, the hallways, and the appointments with students and colleagues. It is a neighborhood called Ridgeview Estates in Lexington, Kentucky. And it is a family made up of a husband, wife, and two teenaged children. The *specificity* of place determines the *spirituality* of place. All of us can wish for or envision a different set of circumstances, but the places we occupy are the realities of our lives. It is *here* that we must pray— where we are. As the places come into view as something more than a blur or a recurring round of dulling routine, they become places where prayer can and should be made.

Second, we must then train ourselves to pray in those places. I confess this is not easy for me. I have had to devise some concrete ways so that I do not forget to pray. I have some "prayer reminders" that call me to pray where I am during the day. Laubach's flash prayers are my mainstay, but I have also added some other things that keep place and prayer connected. For example, I like to use my daily calendar as a prayer book. I use the time walking from my office to my classes as an opportunity to pray for the students whom I will be teaching. I let the noonday siren call me to pray for life as it is unfolding for me. I use the right-hand turn into my subdivision at the end of the day as a call to pray for my neighbors and my family.

I have seen prayer reminders pasted to bathroom mirrors, car dashboards, and telephones. I have seen signs on the back of doors that said, "Don't forget to pray." I have known people who set their watch alarms to "beep" on the hour as a special call to prayer. All of these are simply ways of conditioning the mind and the heart toward prayer. As time passes, we discover that we become less dependent on them. The connection between place and prayer becomes stronger. In these contemporary ways we learn the importance of Jesus giving the Lord's Prayer on the mountain and on the road.

Where is the place in which you spend most of your time during the day? Write the name of that place in the space below.

Who are the people in that place? These may be people who are present most of the time, or they may be people who enter that place temporarily, or who enter that place and your life via the phone. Write down the names or a designation for these people who are part of your primary place.

Finally, select from this list the person who has made the greatest impression on you, and the person who has barely made any impression. On a sheet of paper or in a journal notebook, write a short prayer for each of these persons.

Questions for Discussion
Chapter Two

1. If the idea of praying in ordinary places is new to you, how did this chapter help you better understand this concept?

2. If the idea of praying in ordinary places is not new to you, when and how did you come to know this?

3. What are the "ordinary places" in your day that can become invitations to prayer?

Chapter Three

Prayer: Now?

I confess. I am absentminded. Apparently, it goes with the territory of being a professor. But it hinders more than my teaching; it hinders my praying as well. I know there have been more times than I would like to admit when I have said to someone, "I will pray for you," and then not remembered to do so. The problem was not that I never intended to pray; it was that when my designated prayer time arrived, the promise was forgotten.

One certainly does not have to be a professor to have this problem in prayer. Every time I mention this difficulty, someone will say, "You are telling my story." Together we lament the promised prayers that have gone un-prayed and now lie buried deep in the sea of forgetfulness.

The cure for this disease is near at hand and easy to swallow. It is simply called "praying now." A number of years ago, I began to practice this and it has improved my batting average considerably. Now, when someone comes up to me and says, "Please pray for me"; or, Please pray for _____ ," unless the request is especially confidential or delicate, I will respond, "Would it be OK if we prayed right now?" In all my years of using this approach, I only recall one person saying no.

Prayer Time—Ordinary Time

When Jesus gave the Lord's Prayer, Luke tells us that he had just finished a time of his own private praying. We have already seen that Jesus was in an ordinary place. Now let's add to our picture and realize he was praying at an ordinary time. No bells had rung indicating that the hour for prayer had arrived. There is no indication that the day was a prescribed holy day on the Jewish religious calendar. Jesus simply picked a time and prayed.

This is the model he gave us throughout his lifetime. The Gospels reveal Jesus praying early in the morning and late at night. Luke simplifies the picture to tell us that "Jesus often withdrew to lonely places and prayed" (5:16). Sometimes he would pray briefly, as he did before Lazarus' tomb (John 11:42). At other times he spent hours in prayer, as when he prayed all night before choosing the apostles (Luke 6:12-13). For Jesus, the time might be short or long, but anytime was prayer time.

Through the giving of the Lord's Prayer, Jesus passed along in words what he had demonstrated in deeds. He said, "When you pray. . . ." We could accurately translate the *when* as "whenever." Whenever you pray—night or day, in public or in private, for a brief period or a long time—whenever.

Anyone who has been nurtured in a tradition that contains devotional times will be stretched by this notion. We may have come out of the Roman Catholic tradition in which there are fixed hours and forms for prayer. We may have been reared as Episcopalians with *The Book of Common Prayer* and its Daily Offices of Morning Prayer and Evening Prayer. Or we may have come out of an evangelical Protestantism that closely links praying with the practice of a "quiet time." If so, then expanding prayer to anytime will require some adjustments on our part.

This does not mean we should abandon fixed times for prayer. Such times are "divine appointments" that create essential space in the day to commune with God. They give prayer a focus and intentionality that is necessary. The history of Christian spirituality has consistently

41

affirmed set times of prayer. We need to make and keep these divine appointments.

I meet people all the time who tell me they do not have any special or fixed times for prayer, that they just "pray all day long." I do not doubt their sincerity, but I do question their practice. It does not square with the example of Jesus or that of our predecessors in the faith. I do not know of a single saint in times past who omitted fixed times of prayer. Some of them were very spontaneous, "on-the-go" types, but they still included some time of fixed prayer in their total prayer life.

When Jesus gave the Lord's Prayer, he was in no way abandoning the idea of fixed prayer times. He was simply reminding us that prayer is not limited to or reserved for special times. The goal of the spiritual life is not to have a devotional time, but to live a devotional life. Since life is continuous and comprehensive, it cannot be turned on and off. Life is occurring all the time; therefore, all the time is time for prayer. We might call this "whenever prayer."

Whenever Prayer

First, "whenever prayer" keeps the presence of God continually before us. Who can forget

Brother Lawrence, the little lay monk of the seventeenth century, who left us the classic *The Practice of the Presence of God*? In that small jewel he showed us the sacredness of every hour. He testified that he came to the place where God was as real and dear to him when he was washing dishes in the monastery kitchen as when he was receiving the Eucharist in the cathedral.

His story inspires us because it does not take long in the Christian life to be frustrated with the "gaps"—that is, those blank spaces in the day when we are unaware of God's presence and, seemingly, unaffected by divine influence. We are sort of on "automatic pilot," and at the end of the day we easily see how much of the day was a fog so far as a conscious sense of God's presence is concerned. Something inside us says, *There has to be more to Christianity than these fits of stopping and starting—of moving in and moving out of an awareness of God in our lives.*

I have been challenged and helped by the Quaker writer Thomas Kelly. In his modern-day classic *A Testament of Devotion*, he shares his belief in our ability to live simultaneously on two levels. On one level, we are fully engaged in the events of the day; on another, we are fully engaged in God. This, says Kelly, is one of the magnificent features of the human soul. Kelly calls on us to develop an ability to pray in the midst of the usual moments of our day.

John Wesley had apparently trained himself in the art which Kelly describes. An examination of his diary reveals that he cultivated the habit of checking what he called his "temper of devotion" every hour. By some means, Wesley entered hourly into conscious communion with God. As we read his diary it is clear that he did not withdraw every hour into some holy place or mystical state. Rather, to use Brother Lawrence's phrase, he had learned to "practice the presence of God" while in the midst of routine activity.

I take heart from examples like these. All these people were busy, even Brother Lawrence. Like myself, Thomas Kelly was a professor, was married and had children. John Wesley was a virtual one-man overseer of a movement. Yet, each of these tell the same story: it is possible to close the "gaps" and find increasing continuity of communion between our spirits and the Spirit of God. They challenge me to see that the presence or absence of activity is not the pivot on which prayer turns. Rather, the secret to prayer lies in learning to commune with God in the midst of activity.

How were they able to do this? Brother

Lawrence sheds some light on this question when he tells us that he came to believe it was just as much an act of devotion to pick up a stick so that someone coming along later would not trip over it, as it was to receive Holy Communion. In other words, Brother Lawrence and the others were able to "close the gaps" by seeing all of life as holy. *Anytime is a fit time for prayer* precisely because all time is *kairos*, is God's time. These persons did not divide life up into categories. To them, all life is sacred, all life is to be lived to God's glory.

One of the reasons we have trouble with continuous devotion is because we have made too wide a gulf between the sacred and the secular. Please note, I do not mean between good and evil. Rather, I mean between where we think God is and where we think God is not. God is obviously in quiet times and worshipful moments. But most of us do not live a life that is saturated with such moments and times. More likely ours is a world of noise and activity, of dirty diapers and high-pressure deadlines. Give me the "green pastures and still waters" whenever I can get there. But more than that, give me a sense of God's presence in the midst of my labors. That's the kind of prayer life I need.

If Mother Teresa sees the face of Jesus in the face of a dying person in Calcutta, surely

God's grace can enable me to see the face of Christ in the faces of my students, my friends, my neighbors, my wife, and my children. That is one of the benefits of "whenever prayer."

Morning or Night Prayer?

Second, "whenever prayer" fits the reality of human variations. Each of us can pray, but each of us cannot pray at the same time of day with equal vitality. The fact is, some of us are "morning people" and some of us are "night people." The metabolism of individual persons varies; consequently, alertness also varies from person to person.

Having left this physiological fact out of much of our praying and our thinking about prayer is unfortunate. In nearly thirty years of public ministry, I have seen people struggle to keep awake during sunrise services and others grow weary during late-night "afterglows." I have been in teaching sessions when leaders virtually equated real faith with early-morning prayer. And I have been in other settings where it was perceived that one's faith was validated by the ability to "pray all night."

If we just read the Bible we can be saved from this kind of unnecessary legalism and judgmental attitude. Jesus simply said, "When you pray. . . ." He left the specificity of that "when" to the one praying. Later on, Paul wrote to the Colossians and said, "Devote yourselves to prayer, being watchful and thankful" (Col. 4:2, NIV). The word *watchful* carries the idea of physical alertness, of being awake when we pray. (See also Micah 7:7, Matthew 26:41, and Luke 12:37.) The Colossians passage simply says that we are to build a prayer life in relation to our alertness. And each of us must examine her or his life and determine when that best time of alertness is.

This is not a license for laziness. Even when you determine your best time for prayer, there will be plenty of times when you do not *feel* like praying. Nor is this a license permitting you to omit praying at times other than your best. I am still not a "morning person," but I do not fail to pray in the morning. I just do not pretend to make the weak part of my day carry the weight of my praying. I reserve my strongest praying for when I am strongest.

As I write these words, it has been less than three months since I had another confirmation of what I am saying. One afternoon he stood in my office doorway, asking if I had a few minutes to talk. He wasted no time telling me his prayer life was in the pits. When I asked him to tell me why, he narrated an eighteen-month period of trying to rise early and do his intense praying before sunrise. A year and a half earlier he had been at a prayer school where this was presented as a must in the spiritual life.

But he knew it was not working. Many mornings he tried to pray, only to fall asleep (never mind that he was going to school and working a night job, often staying up until past 1:00 in the morning). Even when he did manage to stay awake, he described it as trying to pray in a fog, with no sense that his prayers were having any effect. He added to this story the fact that ever since his conversion he had struggled to make morning prayer vital.

I have to admit I was impressed that he had given it a try for eighteen months, and I told him so. I also told him that when he combined his metabolism with his school and work schedule, I was not the least bit surprised that early morning prayer was not satisfying or helpful to him.

I asked him when he was most alert. He told me he had always been a "night person." As it turned out, his after-school job was that of a security guard in the evenings. This was a time to unwind some, a time to be pretty much alone, and to be quiet. In between duties, he studied and relaxed as much as he could. I suggested that he move the bulk of his praying to that time. I shared Paul's counsel to be "watchful" in prayer and suggested that these hours seemed to be when he was most alert. I asked him to try this new plan for three weeks and then let me know how that worked for him.

I did not have to wait three weeks. About ten days later he was back in the office. Prayer had come alive for him. "Prayer is the best it's ever been since I became a Christian," he said. But the truth is that prayer had come alive for him because he was praying when he was most alive. Prayer was at its best because he was praying when he was at his best.

Growing up in the Wesleyan tradition, I do not know how many times I heard that John Wesley used to rise and pray at 4:30 or 5:00 in the morning. But the part that was completely left out of the story was the fact that he usually went to bed at 9:30 or 10:00 at night. I can be spiritual on seven hours of sleep too!

Prayer and the Reality of Our Lives

Third, "whenever prayer" fits with reality. I keep a prayer list of sorts, but I am glad that I do not have to wait to pray until I can return to my list. I have a devotional plan, but I am glad I do not have to wait to pray until I can find enough time to execute my plan. Life does not work that way. Jesus said, "When you pray. . . ." And the "whens" are whenever life demands that we stop the presses and storm heaven's gate. Sometimes prayer simply cannot wait.

Jesus prayed like this. When the crowds pressed upon him with their needs, he did not say, "I will certainly pray for you during my quiet time later in the day." No. He prayed at that moment. Prayer life is always inextricably connected to real life.

But here is one insight we must not miss. The instant prayers of Jesus, and even of those who have prayed likewise since him, were not exceptional. They flowed out of the ongoing communion between his spirit and the Spirit of God. Our Lord and the saints of the ages could pray during the storms because they had been praying in the sunshine. They could pray occasionally because they had also been praying continually. It is prayer's "whenever" nature that is the foundation for the special, emergency times—not the other way around.

What is a time you do not normally associate with prayer? Take a few moments to reflect on why you have not used that time for prayer. In the space provided on the next page, write down your impressions.

Then, write out a short prayer that you might pray at that time of the day. Let the prayer be brief enough so you can memorize it. Then for the next three days, remember to pray it during that time of day.

Questions for Discussion
Chapter Three

1. Did you receive any new insights or confirmations from this chapter? If so, write these down on a sheet of paper or in a journal notebook. Why do you feel they are especially important for you right now? If you are participating in a study group, share these insights in your group.

2. What ways might you devise to remind yourself that anytime is a good time to pray? Write down your ideas.

3. Are you a "morning person" or a "night person"? Share in your group (or write in your journal or on a sheet of paper) how the fact that you are a "morning person" or a "night person" has hindered or helped your prayer life. How have you changed your problems into opportunities in this regard?

Chapter Four

Prayer: About *This*?

The audience chuckled when the person asked me, "Do you think it's OK to pray for a parking space?" I had to admit that I could not recall ever having prayed about that, but I could also tell that the person had raised a question that everyone in the group was interested in; namely, the question about prayer's specificity. We all want to know how detailed and "ordinary" our prayers can become before they deteriorate into the trivial.

An examination of the petitions of the Lord's Prayer can help us. When Jesus gave the prayer, he communicated an invitation to pray about the normal things of life. The requests have to do with things we encounter in daily living: physical sustenance, forgiveness when we fail, tolerance of others, strength to resist temptation, and an ability to live above the evils of the world. The prayer does not contain a single desire or detail that is abstract or unrelated to real life.

Where did we get the widespread notion that certain concerns may not be "acceptable" to pray about? I suspect it is rooted in our concept of God. Somehow we have an image of God that says, "God is awfully busy running the universe and does not appreciate being bothered with interruptions about things that don't matter much." And so, many of our prayers have an artificial quality to them. We get so caught up in trying to tell significant or flattering things in prayer that we lose touch with the pressing concerns of our lives.

But this is completely foreign to the picture of God we see both in the example of Jesus and in the teachings of the Gospels. Jesus was touched by and involved in the common issues of daily living. The things that moved people moved him. In fact, this is one of the radical aspects of Christianity. In the pagan religions the gods were safely removed from everyday living. They merely observed, almost like a crowd watching a sporting event on a playing field. Human existence was entertaining, but the gods were not involved in it.

What a contrast we see in Christianity! The Word of God, made flesh and dwelling among us. Jesus Christ coming to live real life on this real planet, experiencing the full range of human emotions and circumstances. Is it any wonder that the prayer Jesus gave us would be consistent with the life he lived?

The Word, Among Us

When the gospel began to spread throughout the world, it addressed itself directly to the issues of life. Not one of Paul's letters, for example, fails to take the grand and general truths of the faith and apply them in some way to the particular needs of the people. In fact, James goes so far as to say, "Faith without works is dead" (James 2:26). Is it any wonder that the prayers of the early church include not only lofty expressions of praise but also earthy petitions that are necessary to keep life on track?

This is the example given us in the Lord's Prayer and it is the revelation of the rest of scripture. We are in relation with God, who monitors the minutest details of life. When we pray, we are invited to pray about those details. I was fascinated years ago by a book entitled *How Much Prayer Should a Hamburger Get?* The title raised an important question, and the book went on to enforce the idea that the details of our lives *are* fit subjects for prayer. The Lord's Prayer makes the same point. It tells us that true prayer embraces the whole of life.

This is not only a clear truth; it is an essential one. In the details of life lies the place where the beauty and power of prayer become apparent. Specificity increases the reality and the relevance of prayer. To be sure, there are times when we pray more generally, because that is the only way we know how to pray at the time. But the more generally we pray, the less able we are to see God at work answering our prayers. When we pray generally and vaguely, there is always the lingering question: But would it have happened anyway? In the long haul God is going to be generally good to everyone. General goodness, however, makes it difficult to discern the direct attention and involvement of God in our lives.

The Specificity of Prayer

When Jesus used the words we translate as "this day" and "daily bread," he was pointing to the specificity of prayer. There is nothing more specific than this particular day—today. In fact, I think of the specificity of my life in terms of each day's responsibilities. Prayer focuses and clarifies the presence and activity of God in the specificity of my life. It does not eliminate the questions; in fact, sometimes it raises questions. But a lifetime of specific prayer yields indisputable evidence that God cares about us.

When police look for fingerprints, they do not take panoramic views; they put the evidence under a microscope. Look at your hands. Etched into your palms and fingertips are tiny lines that make you absolutely unique—distinct from every other human being. Does it make sense to think that God would take the time to work in particulars we can hardly see, and then not care about the other, more significant details of our existence? The lines in my hands cry out to me and say, "If God cares all the way down to this level, everything else is under the shadow of divine loving concern as well."

Nuances and details are likewise at the heart of great sport and art. Major league batters will take batting practice for hours, making minor adjustments in their stance and swing. To the untrained eye, there appears to be little or no difference. But to the professional, a slight shift can improve the batting average significantly.

I am a fair-weather chess player. My strategy is a broad one: Protect the king, no matter what! But when I watch a professional chess match on television, I observe the masters pondering their move of the pawns as much as of their kings. In fact, I have been told that games are won or lost as much in the movement of pawns as in that of knights or bishops.

Great musicians have "style." But style does not mean merely moving up and down the keyboard or playing the correct notes. Style denotes the details in the nuances of the playing. Consequently, a person can tell in an instant whether a piece is Bach or Beethoven. There is no difficulty in distinguishing between Floyd Cramer and Liberace. The details make the difference.

Walking through an art galley, the novice will be able to distinguish the basic differentiation between Realism and Impressionism. But the art expert knows that the major categories can be subdivided into many categories. And again, the criteria are in the subtleties of style, the individual brush strokes here and there. Power, beauty, profundity, and individuality all shine brightest in the details.

The prayer principle is this: Anything that is of concern to you is fair grounds for prayer. The power and beauty of prayer will come shining through in the specificity of your praying. God will cease to be "out there" or "up there" and will come to reside in your everyday life. God will not be Creator only but will become Companion.

Prayer's Purpose

This does not mean that our praying should become a spiritualized form of "give me, get me." The real purpose and value of prayer is intimacy with God, not acquisition from God. Specificity in prayer must never reduce God to a cosmic bellhop. There is a significant difference between selfish praying and specific praying. Jesus' instruction to pray about the daily matters of life is not permission to become self-preoccupied.

In *The Prayers of Jesus* Joachim Jeremias brings out that *Abba* was the Aramaic word from which "Father" is translated in the Lord's Prayer. *Abba* was the term used by small children as their first address to their fathers, much as small children in English-speaking cultures say "Da-da" or "Daddy." By Jesus' day, apparently this was the way in everyday life that an Aramaic-speaking child, whether young or grown, addressed his or her father when speaking to him. By inviting us to refer to God as "*Abba*," Jesus reinforces the intimacy of prayer and turns us away from self-preoccupation. The focus is upon God, who is near, concerned, and interested in all aspects of our lives, just as a parent loves to be involved in a child's total experience of life. We pray to God, who seeks our best and who works for our best in the details of our lives. We are invited to bring everything to God in prayer.

Maxie Dunnam has also helped me by introducing me to the idea of "praying your life." By this he means nothing more or less than inviting God to have presence and influence in the details of my life. This is not selfishness; this is the realization that God is interested and involved in the realities of my existence. Along with my Bible, the hymnal, and devotional books, I also see my pocket calendar as part of my praying. Yes, prayer is more than the details of my day, but it is certainly not less.

In *You Can Pray As You Ought* Arnold Prater tells how this discovery dawned on him. For years, Prater says, he would get up in the morning and, despite a headache and an almost overpowering desire to crawl back into bed, he would instead praise God with flowing words that were sometimes a million miles away from his real feelings. One morning, God seemed to say to him, "Arnold, would you knock it off? I know how you feel and you know how you feel. Would you please talk to me about the things that are really going on in your life?" At first, it seemed strange to begin the day with God by saying, "Lord, you know that my head aches and I'd really rather sleep in, but here I am!" Over time, however, this kind of specificity and honesty made prayer come alive for Arnold Prater.

The Lord's Prayer takes on the beauty and value of an expensive Oriental carpet. The elements of time, place, and specificity weave together to make up the fundamental tapestry of prayer. We cannot ignore any of these dimensions and continue to pray vitally and realistically. The finished product will be as unrepeatable as any artistic masterpiece. It will be as unique as the unrepeatable aspects of our lives. This means that the prayer life of a teenaged girl will be greatly different than her praying when she is a grandmother. Single persons and married persons will pray about different concerns. New Christians will have a different agenda than seasoned veterans in the faith. Like a tapestry, there will be common threads, but they will go in different directions, making different designs.

This truth also contains a dual challenge. It means that we must bring specificity to our praying. But it also means that we must not stand in judgment of the content of another person's prayers. Remember, anything that is of concern to a person is proper content for prayer.

Return with me to the question about praying for a parking place. Although I had to confess that this had never been a high-priority item on my prayer agenda, I sensed it was a reality for the person asking the question. As I probed a little farther, I discovered that the woman who asked had arthritis and it was difficult for her to carry shopping bags very far without pain. This was why she made it a practice to ask God to provide a space as near to the door as possible. Apparently, some of her friends had made fun of her for praying like that. But they did not have arthritis!

When we commit ourselves to specific prayer, we do run some risks. One of the risks is to allow our selfishness to take over and to dwell too much on matters of self-interest. The other danger, however, is to monitor too closely the kinds of things other people pray for. Specificity in prayer can lead us to think, *I never would have prayed for* that! But we must resist the temptation to judge what another person prays for. Mark Spitz, the Olympic swimmer, might never pray for a parking space. Joni Eareckson-Tada, a quadriplegic, might. In praying specifically we must ask the Spirit to preserve us from reducing prayer to self-gratification, and we must ask the Spirit to keep us free from a judgmental attitude.

But there is more. Even after I convince my-self that anything is proper content for prayer, I still have a problem, for I realize how unaware and out of touch I am with the details of my life. Much of my life has been put on "automatic pilot." I have become so accustomed to the routines of my day that I can move from one place to another without noticing anything in between.

I was in a workshop with a nationally known leader in prayer and spiritual life. At one point in the seminar he announced, "We're going for a walk. Just follow me. Don't say a word to anyone. Just walk." And so we did. We walked through the library, out of the building and down the sidewalk. We crossed a street and followed a path that eventually brought us back to our seminar room and our seats. Then the leader began to ask us things like What color was the dress of the receptionist? What kind of bird was singing on the telephone wire? How many people did we meet on our journey?

It did not take long to understand his mes-sage. Then we had thoughts about the times people have said things like, "I waved at you the other day, but you didn't see me." One of the dangers of familiarity is that it works like an anesthetic, dulling our senses and powers of awareness.

A first step for us toward specific praying may be getting back in touch with the specifics of life. You cannot pray about what you do not notice. You cannot ask God to be present and active in the things or events that escape attention. "Praying your life" implies that you are sufficiently in touch with your life to pray meaningfully.

As a means of recapturing some of the "lost territory" of my life, I now commute back and forth to work with the radio turned off. I use these 40–45 minutes a day to let as many details as possible surface in my mind. I then convert those into a prayer. My car has become my "portable hermitage." In addition to my more formal times of devotion, I have found almost another hour a day to pray! That is wonderful.

"Red Time"

Not long ago, I was reading an airline magazine while en route to a meeting. One of the articles in it described "red time." I had never heard of this kind of time before. It is the name of a particular kind of time space that business executives are encouraged to put into their daily calendars and schedules. It is a time free from as much noise as possible, and free from all outside interruptions. It is a time to look beneath the surface of activity and business. It is not time away from the job. Most often, it is time right in the middle of the day. Studies have shown that "red time," among other benefits, increases creativity, the ability to think on one's feet, and the capacity to make beneficial decisions.

As I read that article I thought to myself, *The people of the world are smarter than many people of the church.* In an article that never once mentioned God, "red time" became a call back to the ancient practice of examination and meditation. Suddenly, I was surrounded by "the great cloud of witnesses"—the saints of the ages who have learned that life-influencing communion with God requires space and time to look deeper than the surface. A secular article became a spiritual challenge for me to recover those "mini-retreats" during each day when I can hold up to God every aspect of my life.

One of the practical benefits of this perspective is the way it has changed how I think about interruptions. We have all had the experience of praying about something, when suddenly, uninvited, something else pops into our minds. I remember one time when I was praying intensely for a missionary just to find myself thinking about needing to change the oil in my car. Where did that come from? *And why*, I wondered, *did such things interfere with my praying?*

I no longer look at it that way. When an unsuspected "fly-thought" buzzes around my mind, I fix my attention on it to see why my sub-conscious mind released it. For example, the oil change became a symbol of my need to attend to a detail that would preserve the life of my car, an area of anxiety for me at the time since I lacked funds for either major repairs or a new car.

Praying about interruptions embraces them as windows to greater insight rather than fight-ing them as distractions. In treating them this way, I can give them a look and then move more easily back to the subject I was addressing.

Prayer—about *this*? That is a question we have all asked at one time or another. In giving us the Lord's Prayer, Jesus has told us, "Yes, about 'this'—and about anything else that is in your life." All the way from the majestic, mountaintop issues to the miniscule grains of sand on the seashore of your life. All of it merits a "Dear God" at the beginning and an "Amen" at the end.

Let's personalize what we have been saying. If you have ever thought about whether or not a particular item was all right to mention in your prayers, write down the name of that item. Then, reflect on why you have been hesitant to talk with God about it.

Even if nothing comes to mind, think of a detail of your life about which you have never prayed, or about which you have not prayed in some time. Write it in the space provided, and reflect on how it *could* be an appropriate matter about which to pray.

In the remaining space, write a short prayer about either of the items you have mentioned.

Questions for Discussion
Chapter Four

1. What new insights or confirmations did you receive from this chapter?

2. What is the latest "daily" thing you have made part of your prayer life? How has it made God more real and intimate for you?

3. What ways have you discovered to become more aware of God's presence in the specifics of your life? In a journal notebook or on a separate sheet of paper, write them down as a reminder to yourself.

Chapter Five

Prayer: Like This?

When I was in seminary, a church nearby offered a class on Sunday evening designed to teach persons how to "pray in the Spirit." Closer examination revealed that it was a session where special leaders would utter their prayers and the novices were simply told to repeat what they heard, even if what they heard was an unknown tongue. The assumption was, "There are some folks here who know how to pray. If you want to know how to pray, repeat after them."

Ever since Jesus gave the Lord's Prayer (and even before) people have tried to turn prayer into some kind of magic formula. They have felt, and even taught, that if you could use the right words, use them in the right order, and use them in the right spirit, God was somehow obligated to give exactly what you asked for.

This notion is even older than the contest between Elijah and the prophets of Baal, as recorded in 1 Kings 18. Baalism and most of the other pagan religions of that time considered prayer to be a mystical, magical exercise. And so, the prophets of Baal recited their prayers and marched around the altar, all according "to the book." But no fire fell. They shouted and they danced. They did everything they were supposed to do to get results. But nothing happened.

When Elijah's turn came he, by contrast, prayed a short prayer (a verse and a half long in scripture). And the fire of God fell and consumed the offering on the altar, the altar itself, the ground around the altar, and the water which had been used to soak everything. A few moments of true prayer accomplished what hours of "prayer magic" had been unable to do.

As ancient as this experience is, we have seen a contemporary resurgence of it in our own generation. At the extremes of prayer the "name it and claim it" movement arose with the heretical idea that whatever we speak somehow obligates God to answer immediately and to answer exactly as we have prayed. As if that were not enough, some advocates even took it farther to teach that this kind of "naming" includes requests for lots of money, for big cars, fabulous homes, and other spectacular displays of wealth.

When Jesus gave the Lord's Prayer, he was

teaching against every notion that would make prayer magical or complex. He watched the Pharisees pray long, elaborate prayers, mistakenly thinking they would be heard for their "much speaking" (see Matthew 6:7 and Luke 18:9-14). The "much speaking" referred directly to the pagans; however, that is the point in the Gospels.

The Jews had fallen into the same thing. They began to believe that even the "religious people" can affect the outcome of prayer merely by their "much speaking." Within a generation of Jesus' death, the Gnostics would try to convince people that secret, hidden knowledge was necessary to pray correctly.

Genuine Prayer: The Heart's Desire

By contrast, the Lord's Prayer is remarkable both for its brevity and its simplicity. In the New International Version it numbers just 52 words in Matthew's account and 34 words in Luke. All New Testament scholars I know take this as one of the ways Jesus used to un-complicate prayer and free it from the notion that "long is better."

Likewise, the Lord's Prayer emancipates praying from the notion that complexity is better. The prayer contains short, understandable, everyday words. And it contains words that were given in plain view. No secret knowledge or going behind a curtain to get the magic formula here. Everything is put in the open. Through the Lord's Prayer Jesus is teaching us to let our hearts rather than our vocabulary be the foundation of our praying.

I have always been fascinated by the fact that Jesus gave the Lord's Prayer in response to the request "Lord, teach us to pray." Here is the open admission on the part of the disciples that they did not know how to pray, or at least that they could stand some improvement in their prayer life. Jesus accepted this request at face value and went on from there. Every time a person expresses embarrassment at his or her prayer life—or the lack of it—I derive great joy from telling the person that he or she has just perfectly fulfilled the qualifications for becoming a praying person.

This was demonstrated most clearly to me in a church in west Texas. In the sermon, I had said words similar to the ones I have just written. At the conclusion of the service, one of the men in the congregation came up to me, looked me squarely in the eye and said, "God, I don't even know how to pray."

I responded to him by saying, "Well, if you would just slow that sentence down a little, it would be a prayer." He looked at me as if I had come from another planet. I continued, "See what I mean? Just slow it down a little: 'God, I don't even know how to pray.' Sounds like a prayer to me." He looked at me then with genuine amazement and said, "Yeah, I guess it does." With that, he reached out to shake my hand and asked me to sit down in the pew with him and pray that God would take that simple beginning and teach him to pray.

One cannot get more basic than that. That is exactly where Jesus started in giving the Lord's Prayer—with basics and with people who did not think they knew how to pray, with people who neither knew nor cared about complexity or length of prayers. If all you know is that you want to commune with God, you have satisfied the only requirement for a vital prayer life. Your heart's desire is the only prerequisite for vital praying.

If that sounds like good news, listen again; it gets even better! The reason Jesus grounded prayer life in desire is because he knew that God has placed within every person a desire for communion and communication. Theologians have called it "the God-shaped vacuum in the human heart." What this means is that each person is created to pray and each person wants to pray. And the wonderful thing is that Jesus gave a prayer that touches us right at that place and leads us on from there.

The Lord's Prayer is so simple that it can be memorized by children. Yet, it is so profound that a person can spend a lifetime exploring its message. I have a friend who can barely read, but he knows the Lord's Prayer. And I have other friends with Ph.D. degrees who know the prayer. They all find it moving and meaningful.

Simplicity of Prayer

Simplicity. That is what this is all about. How unfortunate that some in our age have falsely equated the word *simple* with *simplistic*. The longer I live and the more I learn, the more deeply I believe that the mark of a truly intelligent person is the ability to communicate simply. Jesus is the master teacher of prayer. He could use 34 simple words to tell us something that would provide challenge for a lifetime. Indeed, the Lord's Prayer has challenged persons and congregations through the centuries. Not long ago, I decided to do a more in-depth study of the Book of Proverbs. As I began my journey, looking at the book as a whole and doing some commentary reading, I noted that one writer said the power and endurance of the proverbs is their remarkable ability to teach the deep lessons of life in short phrases. He took some of the proverbs and showed how in their brevity they taught the same lessons as more lengthy passages in the writings of the great philosophers.

The same is true of the Lord's Prayer. Volumes have been written about it, but it stands on its own with its brevity and simplicity. It cries out to me to ground my own praying in the same kind of simplicity.

There are some reasons why I think this is so. For one thing, I have noticed that the closer life gets to the core, the less wordy it becomes. When we are most deeply moved, we often say, "I am speechless." When we are in immediate danger, we cry, "Look out!" In either case, we could choose to describe the event in verbose detail, but at those moments words would only get in the way.

The Wordlessness of Prayer

The same is true of prayer. There are times when vocabulary fails to touch the nerve of what is going on in our lives. There are times when words get in the way. In the simplicity of our praying, our deepest feelings are allowed to stand on their own, without unnecessary explanation or interpretation.

Joy was dying of cancer. In the earliest times during our visits we had chatted about this, that, and the other. Joy was a very interesting person and full of life. But as the time of her death drew nearer, our visits became less verbal. In fact, speaking became more and more of a chore for her. The last time I saw her was at the airport where she was about to be put into an air ambulance and taken to a cancer hospital for one last, experimental treatment. Despite my desire as her pastor to say something to her that would help sustain her, all I could get out was "Joy, it's OK." With a look of understanding, she took my hand and answered, "I know."

Just five words exchanged between us, and yet I still consider that to be one of the deepest conversations I have ever had about the spiritual life and God's reality. Since that time, there have been other occasions to remind me that simplicity often reflects the depth of living.

The hymn writer puts it like this:

> There is a place of quiet rest,
> near to the heart of God.

"Quiet rest." A place that does not require "much speaking" in order for there to be communion and communication. "Near to the heart of God." Thirty-four words in the Lord's Prayer that last a lifetime.

On a more practical level, the simplicity of the Lord's Prayer releases us from worrying about what to say while we are trying to pray. As I conduct prayer workshops around the country, people keep telling me, "Sometimes I worry so much about whether I am saying it right that I lose track of what it is I am trying to say." Simplicity frees us from that concern. Jesus is inviting us to talk with God in words that do not have to be checked in a dictionary or verified by a thesaurus.

When I began to study prayer as a professional and vocational pursuit, I was taken aback by the discovery that the deepest prayer is wordless prayer. This is the collective witness of the saints of the ages. At the time I first encountered the idea, I could not bring myself to believe it. I had cut my teeth and formed my mind on the importance of the *spoken* word, at least "spoken" in the heart, if not actually aloud. Wordlessness at first seemed like emptiness. I did not realize I was equating wordlessness with nothingness.

But at the same time, I have learned that listening to those who have made the journey before us is a good idea. Since so many of the saints placed importance on wordless prayer, there had to be a reason, and I wanted to know what that reason was.

I do not mean to imply that I have the complete answer. But I have come to a place where more and more of my own praying is without carefully crafted and spoken words. I have discovered that many of the things I want and need to pray about defy description. How can I put into words everything I feel or think about my wife? How do I fully pray my dreams for children who will soon be leaving home? What are the words to describe a vocational crisis or uncertainty about the future? Where are the words to tell God everything going on after a dear friend has died?

The saints placed primary emphasis on wordlessness in prayer because they knew that every language has its limitations but prayer is limitless. So I feel totally at ease using words when words suffice. And I feel an increasing liberty to let my words cease when they are no longer adequate. There *is* "a place of quiet rest" where words are unnecessary.

The Space of God's Speaking

Finally, I believe simplicity in prayer is important because it creates the space wherein

God can also speak. When I get caught up in my "many words," I sometimes find that the time I have set aside for prayer has been consumed by my doing all the talking. From real-life experience I know there is nothing more boring and unproductive than a one-way conversation.

Prayer is both speaking *and* listening. As I use an economy of words I redeem time to listen, and in so doing, I make prayer the dialogue it was intended to be. I had not been a Christian very long before I ran across John B. Coburn's word that "prayer is response to God." That told me God is the one who speaks first. When I pray, I am always coming in second. Now I add to that the idea that in prayer God wants and needs to have the last word as well. I do not pray to hear myself speak; rather, I pray in order that I may hear God speak. Simplicity of words increases that dimension of prayer.

Rosalind Rinker did the Christian world a great service when she reminded my generation that prayer is nothing more than "conversing with God." It is two friends talking together—with words and without words. We are free forever from thinking that prayer is beyond us if we do not know theological language or Elizabethan English. We are liberated from the prison that would equate vital prayer with complexity and length.

I believe that when Jesus gave the Lord's Prayer, he had one ultimate purpose in mind. He wanted to leave the disciples with one overarching impression—the impression that "I can pray." Likewise, as I preach and teach about prayer, I have no greater joy than to help people make the same discovery. That is my purpose in writing this book.

Prayer—who? me? Yes, *you*! Prayer—now? Yes, right now! Prayer—here? Yes, no better place than right here! Prayer—about *this*? Of course, everything is proper content for prayer! Prayer—like *this*? You bet! And in words that let your heart shine through.

I invite you to get your favorite translation of the Bible and a blank sheet of paper. On one side of the paper, write out either Matthew's or Luke's version of the Lord's Prayer (found in Matthew 6:9-13 or Luke 11:2-4). On the other side of paper, write out your own paraphrase of the prayer, putting its ideas into words you are most comfortable in using.

Questions for Discussion
Chapter Five

1. What insights and spiritual discoveries have you come to through your paraphrasing of the Lord's Prayer?

2. If you are in a study group, invite each person in the group to share his or her paraphrase of the Lord's Prayer. What insights are you able to give and receive from reading your paraphrase and listening to that of others in the group?

3. Have you discovered any other benefits to "simple" prayer in addition to those mentioned in this chapter?

4. In what ways has your study of the Lord's Prayer aided your sense of confidence regarding you own prayer life?

Chapter Six

Ready To Go!

I originally intended to end this book with the previous chapter, but doing that did not seem right. Then I realized that if I have accomplished the purpose of exposing and dealing with some primary obstacles to prayer, it only stands to reason that some word should be given about the use of the Lord's Prayer in actual praying.

Jesus gave the Lord's Prayer so we could pray more effectively. It not only releases us from some of the hurdles, the obstacles, that can bog us down in prayer, it also reveals the motivation for true prayer. Most of all, the Lord's Prayer is an invitation to pray. In previous chapters the way has been marked to overcome certain obstacles to prayer. We are now ready to examine praying according to the plan given us by Jesus in the Lord's Prayer.

Jesus said that God delights in giving "good gifts" to those who ask. I have come to see that the Lord's Prayer is one of those "good gifts" and that it came in response to the disciples' willingness to ask. In this chapter I want to look at some of the good gifts that are contained in the prayer. In the "Additional Resources" section following this chapter, I have listed some of my favorite resources for understanding and practicing prayer.

The Gift of Perspective: The Upward Look

First of the good gifts given in the Lord's Prayer is the gift of perspective. Prayer is more than a way of talking to God and listening to God. Prayer is a way of looking at life. In fact, prayer *is* a way of life. As we pray, our insight is expanded and our vision is clarified.

How many times have you heard someone say, "I don't know why I didn't see it. It was right in front of me all the time." The person may be talking about a literal object, or "it" may refer to an idea or a decision. This is simply a way of saying it is easy to lose perspective.

Prayer is God's gift to help us maintain perspective by providing us with a look at life from three essential points of view: the upward look, the inward look, and the outward look.

First, prayer gives us "the upward look." All prayer begins with God because life is centered and founded in God. "Our Father" is more than a polite means of address; it is a profound statement about the source of life's meaning and purpose. And, as we have seen, this is an address of intimacy, centered in the belief that God cares about the totality of our lives. It is from our *Abba* that we receive and it is to our *Abba* that we request. All of life is resourced from and referenced to God.

"Thy kingdom come, thy will be done on earth" makes sense only if we believe that there is a "higher way"—a way that transcends the sensory and chronological aspects of our lives.

The final phrase of the Lord's Prayer, "for thine is the kingdom, and the power, and the glory forever and ever" only amplifies this belief. The phrase closes the prayer for us with our vision firmly fixed upon the eternal dimension.

In giving us the Lord's Prayer, Jesus is saying that for life to work as it should, it must have the upward look. Jesus came to provide a perspective of the kingdom of God. Prayer is God's gift which gives us that larger vision. Prayer enables us to become Kingdom people— God's people. Jesus described it as having "eyes to see" and "ears to hear."

Leslie Weatherhead illustrated this best for

me in his parable of the Divine Weaver, from his *Time for God.* Serving as a missionary in India for a number of years, he often saw the large looms and the weavers creating Oriental rugs. From his perspective as an observer, a rug on the loom appeared to be a meaningless tangle of threads. There was no discernible pattern, and certainly nothing of the beauty which made many of these rugs masterpieces.

But the fact is, he was looking at the back side of the rug. The loom was set up in such a way that only the weaver could see the precious picture that was emerging as the threads were pulled through the fabric. Every now and then, says Weatherhead, a weaver would invite him to step around to what was really the front side of the loom. The movement was transformational, often breathtaking.

Sometimes life looks like the back side of a loom. A day's circumstances seem as disconnected as the threads on the underside of an Oriental rug. We are hard pressed to see any pattern or purpose to it all. Prayer is the Divine Weaver's invitation to step around to what is really the front side of the loom, to the eternal side of life. And the movement is transformational, often breathtaking. The upward look of prayer reveals the real meaning of life.

In giving us the Lord's Prayer, Jesus was

inviting us to step around the loom and see life from the perspective of heaven. True prayer is God's invitation to see life through God's eyes and to set the circumstances of life in their larger context. We need this perspective if we are to see our lives as more than a disconnected sequence of random events.

I think this is why Jesus withdrew so often to pray. From the moment of his baptism until the day of his crucifixion, he was locked in a life–and–death struggle with evil principalities and people. It would have been so easy to see only the tangles of life. Bitterness and cynicism are only a heartbeat away at that point. But through prayer, Jesus was able to put it all into perspective. And as he looked at the cross itself, he was able to say, "It was for this that I came into the world" (refer to John 16:27-28).

Two thousand years later, skeptics still try to write off his life as a waste. But they are standing on the wrong side of the loom. Their conclusion is constricted because their perspective is limited. By contrast, those who have the upward look of prayer have been caught up in the same transforming vision of who Jesus is and why he came to the earth. Prayer is God's invitation to move to the front side of the loom.

Prayers of praise and prayers for insight are related to the upward look. One term for it is *consideration*—to look deeply, to ponder, to dwell in the presence of God until you begin to transcend the limitations of your own mind. Hugh of Saint Victor called this kind of meditative prayer "piercing the core of a particular truth." He taught that God gives us the capacity to go beneath the surface of our lives to see the greater realities.

The Lord's Prayer, however, is not magic. The upward look does not always come quickly and easily. It is not always given through ecstatic experiences. The saints have known extended periods of dryness and lack of direction. But like the children of Israel, they wandered with God, believing that in God lies the real meaning of life. Even as the spokes of a wheel find their center in the hub, so, too, the upward look of prayer keeps life centered in its Source.

The Gift of Perspective:
The Inward Look

Second, the Lord's Prayer gives us "the inward look." Prayer is not only getting in touch with God, it is getting in touch with one's self and one's own life. It is God's gift to help us see the things that really matter. And we all know how easy it is to be self-deceived.

The Lord's Prayer reveals life's essentials. In its verses we see the need for daily sustenance, for forgiveness and the ability to forgive others, for strength to resist the temptations of life, and for the power to rise above the evils that can entrap and destroy us. When I think of how many specifics can be put under each of these categories, my appreciation for the Lord's Prayer increases. And when I think of how many aspects of my life fall into one of these areas, I see how "real" this prayer is in addressing life as I live it.

Here is one place where prayer and psychology interact. Through prayer, God stimulates all my mental processes. I can "see" myself and my needs more clearly. I am enabled to pray about these personal dimensions. The inward look does not result in selfishness but in clarification. Such clarification may lead me to confession of sin, to reconciliation with others, to deep cries for strengthening, or to any number of other prayers or actions. The inward look of prayer leads, over time, to the transformation of self through enlightenment, obedience, and becoming more Christlike in character and conduct.

The Lord's Prayer calls me to regularly take stock of my life and to call upon God's grace to enable me to live a truly Christian life in each of these areas. The inward look of the prayer is designed to "get to the heart of the matter." And Jesus told us that it is from the "heart" that the issues of life flow.

Prayers of recollection and self-examination are related to the inward look. One word for it is *humility*. Prayers of the inward look are one of the best ways of determining who is in charge here. They remind us of the Lordship of Christ. They are prayers that reflect the spirit of the hymn which says, "Take my life, and let it be consecrated, Lord, to thee." In giving us the Lord's Prayer, Jesus was giving us the gift of seeing ourselves aright.

The Gift of Perspective: The Outward Look

Third, the Lord's Prayer gives us "the outward look." The prayer was given in public to the crowds, and it uses plural terms. In taking this approach, Jesus made it clear that the full meaning of life is not contained in getting, having, and consuming. It is found in giving and in serving. Saint Teresa of Ávila taught that prayer which does not move us to love our neighbor is not true prayer.

The outward look is fostered through a sense of community. *Our* and *us* are key words of true prayer and of true Christianity. Prayer levels life, causing everyone to stand on equal ground. I cannot pray for myself correctly without having that same self radically connected to others. It is "our" daily bread. It is "our" trespasses. Lead "us" not into temptation. Deliver "us" from evil.

Prayer reminds me that if I want to have, I must also be willing to give. If there is something I need, it is also something you need. If I ask it of God for myself, I must also ask it of God for you. Prayer is the realization of Paul's reminder that "If one member suffers, all suffer together. . .; if one member is honored, all rejoice together" (1 Cor. 12:26).

We have just passed through the decade of the eighties, that decade when the term *Yuppie* was added to our vocabulary. The eighties were by no means the first decade during which selfishness reigned; it was just the first one that declared it to be a way of life. More openly and blatantly than in other times, the eighties made conspicuous consumption, "looking out for number one," and "name it and claim it" the surest way to "make the world your oyster."

But selfishness has within itself a fatal flaw. Its only option is eventually to become self-consuming. Therefore selfishness has a short life span so far as a controlling philosophy is concerned. There are encouraging signs in the opening of the nineties that many people are beginning to see through the façade and look for a way of life that is more authentic and satisfying. For example, a recent issue of my college's alumni magazine defined *success* as "having a positive impact on a significant number of people."

The Lord's Prayer is the prayer for advancing this definition, for in it is the gift of the outward look. Those who pray this way will lay their self-centeredness at the feet of Jesus, will take the name "servant." Outward-look praying will reveal that "to whom much has been given, much will be required" (Luke 12:48).

The first gift of the Lord's Prayer is the gift of perspective. In each of its dimensions, the Lord's Prayer provides the perspective we desperately need. Most of all, it provides the perspective for doing God's will "on earth as it is in heaven."

The Gift of Plan

The second great gift that Jesus gave us in the Lord's Prayer is that of plan. Almost all biblical scholars agree that Jesus intended the prayer more as a model for prayer than as an actual prayer itself. To be sure, we can pray it just as it is written, and many of us do that each week in public and in private worship. But more significantly than the words themselves is the grand plan for praying that emerges.

I like to think of the Lord's Prayer as a pattern. It gives the basic form of prayer. Those who sew know that one pattern can be used in an almost unlimited number of ways. Even when following the basic pattern, there is possible an amazing amount of personalization and specificity. The color and texture of the cloth is different. The stitching and detail work varies widely. The end result is clothing that fits and accentuates the individual who wears it.

So, too, in prayer Jesus has given us a pattern. But we are left—even invited—to fill in the particulars. Over the years, I have been amazed by how people have used the Lord's Prayer as a basic pattern, yet the finished product has been unique and unrepeatable. I still recall a worship service in our seminary chapel years ago. During the pastoral prayer, it dawned on me that the worship leader was really using the Lord's Prayer as her pattern. I peeked! And sure enough, she had her Bible open throughout the prayer. When she finished, she quietly closed it and sat down. Let me use my recollection of that experience to describe more fully the gift of plan that Jesus gives us.

Our Father. She began by acknowledging the reality and presence of God in the service, and our being one in our desire to worship. Her words helped us center in the sure presence of the Lord, and they served to remind us that we were not worshiping as a collection of individuals but as the Body of Christ.

The tone of her prayer communicated the *Abba* dimension we have referred to (see pages 11, 59–60). By her prayer we were drawn toward God, who invites us to pray, who comes near when we pray, and who is willing and able to answer our prayers. Likewise, the worship leader reinforced the *Abba* concept with a note of confidence in God's presence and in God's desire to be at work in our lives.

When we pray, we need to focus our attention on the presence of God, until that presence becomes real and influential. Sometimes this can happen relatively quickly; at other times, we need to linger at this point in the pattern for some time before we are actually aware of God in our midst.

At the same time, we need to remind ourselves that we never pray alone. We may pray in private, but even then we are praying in community. We would be amazed if we could see how many others are praying at exactly the moment we are praying. We need to begin our prayers in a way that moves this sense of community to the forefront of consciousness.

Who art in heaven. Our worship leader used this part of the pattern to focus on the security and confidence we can have in God. To say that God is in heaven does not imply absence from earth. Rather, it says, "God is in the right place, doing the right things." God is not capricious or inconsistent, nor is God one who may or may not be there when we pray. God *is* in heaven, *is* in charge. No matter when we pray, we can count on that.

To pray "Who art in heaven" elevates my confidence and trust. I know that I will shortly be making various petitions to God. Before I launch into that aspect of prayer, I need to be aware that God is indeed in heaven, ready and willing to do more for me than I can ever ask for or think of.

Hallowed be thy name. In her praying, our leader moved us into a time of praise and celebration, calling us to lift up our hearts to the Holy One, the One above whom there is no other.

Praise is the oil that enables us to slip free of an earthbound perspective and to escape the grasp of a wrenching need. Often in prayer we need to come to a halt in the throne room of prayer, calling out the many names of God, and in doing so remind ourselves that we are in contact with the I Am of all life. As we enter into the aspect of praise, we feel our souls take wings and rise above our circumstances.

Thy kingdom come, thy will be done. Our worship leader used words that reminded us that life is not made up of a random series of disconnected events, that God, Who Is, is the God who has a plan, a desire, and a will. Our prayer leader guided us to the place of seeing that divine will takes precedence over any human desire or request. She challenged us through her praying to come to the place where we would open ourselves to the Divine Voice.

This, too, is important in prayer. As we prepare to offer up our requests, it is essential to remember that we are not praying in order to get God to rubber-stamp our petitions. Instead, we are praying in order to get God's perspective on the things we are praying for. The Lord's Prayer in no way restricts our permission to pray specifically. That is made clear in the verses that follow the Lord's Prayer in Luke and in Matthew. But what is equally clear is that our requests must be set in the larger context of the kingdom or reign of God and offered in the spirit of Jesus who said in Gethsemane, "Abba, Father, . . . not what I want, but what you want" (Mark 14:36).

Give us this day our daily bread. Our prayer

leader spoke to God about the needs of the community, the needs of the day, the needs for sustenance. The list in her prayer petition went beyond food, but the message was clear: we are given the privilege of offering up to God the details of our lives. I remember that she also used this section of the pattern in the Lord's Prayer to thank God that we do not have to get everything said at one time—that we would be back tomorrow, and again, and again, asking God's will to be done in the details of our existence. She reminded us to be thankful that God never grows weary of receiving requests about the particulars of our lives.

Forgive us our trespasses. In the prayer we next moved from *things* to *people.* First, to an awareness of our own imperfections and the need to experience God's forgiveness. Then, into the knotted-up relationships that need to be healed and reconciled. In keeping with the spirit of the Lord's Prayer, our worship leader's prayer also challenged us to remember that our sense of personal forgiveness is in proportion to our willingness to forgive others.

Lead us not into temptation. Then she took us into the holy of holies, into the private places and the personal struggles. Through her own vulnerability she moved us to ask God to deliver us from every evil—actual and potential—that was presently swirling in and around us and threatening to undo us. Reflecting the spirit of the phrase, she instilled the sure confidence that God will never allow us to be tempted beyond what we are able to bear. This section of her prayer ended with the grand reminder that God's grace is sufficient.

For thine is the kingdom. The pastoral prayer landed on the solid rock of assurance. We had come full circle. In the middle of the prayer we had indeed entered into the uncertain areas and named our deepest fears, but we had completed the journey in the face of God's eternal power and glory.

I hope this extended description has been enough to help you see how the Lord's Prayer leads to an amazing variety as we use it from day to day. There are times in my daily devotions when I will simply open my Bible and use the lines of the Lord's Prayer as stimulators to a whole range of praying within the various categories of the prayer itself. It always works. The few words of the Lord's Prayer are like a knothole in a high, wooden fence. In peering through the small space, we catch a vision of a wider world. Jesus was giving us a precious gift in passing on the Lord's Prayer as a grand plan for our own specific praying.

The Gift of Prayer in Our Hearts

Third, Jesus gave us the great gift of hiding the prayer in our hearts for use at anytime. As we hide the words of the Lord's Prayer in our hearts as the living word of God, it remains active in us throughout the day. Depending on the situation we are facing, we may find a phrase of it rising to consciousness and calling us to prayer.

Not long ago I was struggling with a relationship. Feelings of resentment were building within me toward another person. Suddenly, it was as if God had put a "filter" between that person and me. The filter was simply the words *Forgive us our trespasses, as we forgive those who trespass against us.* Without any additional impressions, the Holy Spirit had set the agenda for my praying in that moment. In other of life's struggles, different portions of the Lord's Prayer have surfaced as guiding lights to me.

A Precious Gift

A television commercial for jewelry says, "Give the gift that keeps on giving." Prayer is like that. It is valuable not only in itself and in the moment it is given but also over and over again.

The Lord's Prayer is valuable in its own right, but even more so as it is pondered, and as its phrases become an almost continuous prayer from deep within. Such prayer can be at the level of mental reflection, or it can become the cry of our lips. It can be hidden in the heart, or expressed in the congregation. The preciousness of the gift of the Lord's Prayer lies in the universality of its use. And so we pray with millions of Christians around the world,

"Abba."

The Lord's Prayer is indeed a precious gift. With the obstacles cleared out of the way, the beauty of the prayer shines through even more clearly. It is there waiting to inform the substance and structure of our praying, and to inspire the spirit of our praying. The Lord's Prayer can stand on its own as a prayer, or it can serve to liberate our thoughts and feelings into an expanded experience. The pattern is there. What we do with it is without limit.

The disciples set all this in motion with their request of Jesus, "Lord, teach us to pray." In giving us the Lord's Prayer, Jesus has fully met that request, and he has done it in a way we can never forget.

May I suggest that you conclude your reading of this book with a prayer experience akin to the Lord's Prayer? It's easy. Just begin by saying,

"*Abba.* Our Father. . . ."

Questions for Discussion
Chapter Six

1. The "good gifts" of the Lord's Prayer as presented in this chapter are the gifts of perspective (the upward look, the inward look, the outward look), the gift of plan, and the gift of prayer in our hearts. Which of these "good gifts" touched you the most? Why?

2. Have you found other "good gifts" from studying and using the Lord's Prayer in your regular prayer time?

3. If studying this book in a group: As a suggested closing to your small-group experience, have someone read aloud each of the phrases of the Lord's Prayer, one at a time. Then allow time between each phrase for anyone who desires, to personalize and particularize the phrase as the leader mentioned in the chapter did in the worship service.

For individual study: Write down each phrase of the Lord's Prayer. Then write down any insights or other prayer phrases that come to you as you spend time praying and meditating on each phrase.

Additional Resources

If I have accomplished my purpose in writing this book, you are now ready to engage in further study of prayer. In fact, your reading of this book was probably not the first exploration you have made into this important dimension of the Christian life.

What follows in this section is a brief, selected list of resources that I believe will help you continue your journey of prayer enrichment. I have added a few comments about each resource so that you can get an idea about its focus and significance. Check with your local public or college library or your local bookstore to find these helpful books on prayer.

Maxie Dunnam, *The Workbook of Living Prayer* and *The Workbook of Intercessory Prayer* (The Upper Room). I do not know of any two better resources on prayer. The material in each chapter is excellent, but even that is enriched by the interactive workbook format.

Harry Emerson Fosdick, *The Meaning of Prayer*. Of all my books on prayer, this is my favorite. Reading it years ago helped prayer come alive for me. Fosdick combines a daily-reading format with more lengthy weekly reflections. The book can also be read straight through, if you prefer.

Frank C. Laubach, *Prayer: The Mightiest Force in the World*. This contemporary classic will help you cultivate a life of prayer, in addition to fixed times of prayer. It is a gem in connecting our ordinary circumstances with our praying.

Brother Lawrence, *The Practice of the Presence of God* (available in the Great Devotional Classics series, The Upper Room; also available in Spanish under the title *Practicando la Presencia de Dios*). This historic classic, perhaps more than any other, can help us understand how to make prayer a way of life.

Thomas Kelly, *A Testament of Devotion*. This contemporary classic helps us move prayer into our daily living, showing how the spiritual life sensitizes us to the needs of those around us.

Reginald Johnson, *Celebrate, My Soul.* This volume helps us see the connection between our personality and our spirituality. It contains a wealth of insight into building a prayer life in harmony with one's temperament.

Kenneth Leech, *True Prayer.* Kenneth Leech utilizes the Lord's Prayer, showing how the prayer itself is a model for our praying. This is one of the best expositions of the Lord's Prayer I have ever read.

Donald G. Bloesch, *The Struggle of Prayer.* Taking a more theological approach, the author grounds us in solid, biblical principles of prayer while acknowledging that prayer is not always easy.

Donald Demaray, *How Are You Praying?* I consider this book one of the best overviews on prayer. It covers a wide variety of personal and corporate issues related to prayer.

Rueben P. Job and Norman Shawchuck, *A Guide to Prayer for Ministers and Other Servants* and *A Guide to Prayer for All God's People.* These two prayer books by the Upper Room (Upper Room Books), each containing a year's worth of material, can ground your spiritual life in meaningful, daily experiences. Each book includes a rich anthology of readings that fit the selected weekly theme and suggested scripture readings based on the Common Lectionary.

John Baillie, *A Diary of Private Prayer*. This contemporary classic contains thirty-one days of morning and evening prayers. The prayers themselves are amazingly insightful and will lead you to experience the wide range of issues and concerns for which you can pray.

Evelyn Christenson and Viola Blake, *What Happens When Women Pray?* This contemporary best seller has helped many women establish a meaningful prayer life. Its principles are equally valuable for men.

Teresa of Avila, *The Way of Perfection*. In this historic classic, Teresa describes prayer as the chief means of advancing in the spiritual life. In addition to its majestic portrayals, this piece also contains practical information to enrich prayer.

John Killinger, *Prayer: The Act of Being with God*. For those who appreciate variety in prayer, this book contains suggestions for numerous different ways to pray.

George A. Buttrick, *Prayer*. For those who desire a solid biblical and theological foundation for praying, this book is unsurpassed. It has achieved the status of a contemporary classic.

C. S. Lewis, *Letters to Malcolm, Chiefly on Prayer.* As the title suggests, this book utilizes a correspondence motif to deal with many subjects related to prayer.

The writings of E. Stanley Jones have been among the most instructive for my own prayer life. Among my favorites are *How to Pray; The Way;* and *Abundant Living.* Abingdon Press has kept some of this author's key writings in print. Check to see which titles are currently available.

Frank Whaling, ed., *John and Charles Wesley* (in The Classics of Western Spirituality series, Paulist Press). No single volume better communicates Wesleyan spirituality than this. Within it are numerous insights into prayer.

About the Author

Steve Harper is Professor of Spiritual Formation and Wesley Studies at Asbury Theological Seminary in Wilmore, Kentucky, and Adjunct Professor at Lexington Theological Seminary. A native of Texas, Dr. Harper is an elder in the Northwest Texas Conference of The United Methodist Church. He has served as an evangelist, as pastor to churches in Texas and in Kentucky, and continues to preach as well as to lead spiritual life retreats and conferences. He is a graduate of McMurry College in Abilene, Texas (B.A.), of Asbury Theological Seminary (M.Div.), and of Duke University (Ph.D.).

An active churchman, he serves on the Board of Reference of the National Prayer Committee and on the Board of Advisors of The Disciplined Order of Christ. He is a member of the American Academy of Religion and of the Society of John Wesley Scholars. He is a certified tutor in the Literacy Volunteers of America and is active in the local literacy program in Lexington, Kentucky.

Dr. Harper was general editor of the Victor Books series on Spiritual Formation. Among his many published books is *Devotional Life in the Wesleyan Tradition*, published by The Upper Room.